ACTION + LEADERSHIP
JOURNAL

APPROACHABLE LEADERSHIP WORKSHOP

SUPPORT.
CONNECT.
THRIVE.

> TO ORDER ADDITIONAL COPIES
>
> To inquire about single or quantity orders of
>
> *The Approachable Leadership Action + Leadership Journal*
>
> Email us at Journal@ApproachableLeadership.com

VISIT US ONLINE http://ApproachableLeadership.com

Copyright ©2017 by Approachable Leadership. All rights reserved. Approachable Leadership® is a Registered Trademark.

No part of this book may be reproduced or transmitted in any form and by any means without prior written permission of the publisher, except in the case of brief quotations in book reviews and critical articles.

Published by Approachable Leadership.

FIRST EDITION

Printed in the United States of America.

ISBN: 978-0-9638554-9-7

THIS JOURNAL BELONGS TO:

If found please return to

_____

_____

_____

IMPORTANT NOTE
See pages 19-21 for some helpful hints on getting the most out of your *Action + Leadership Journal*

EVERYDAY LEADERS

your turn!

#ApproachableLeadership

Everyday Leaders

Your Leader? _____

Why? _____

Two behaviors you admire? _____

_____

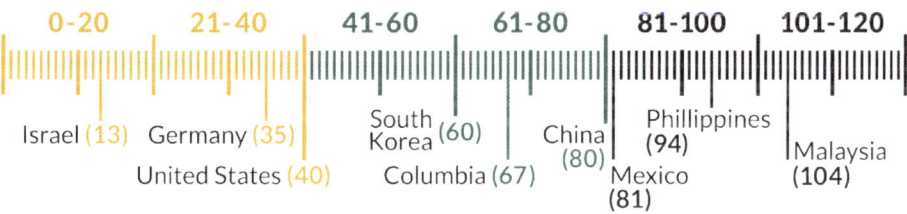

0-20	21-40	41-60	61-80	81-100	101-120

Israel (13) Germany (35) South Korea (60) China (80) Phillippines (94) Malaysia (104)
United States (40) Columbia (67) Mexico (81)

Hofstede's Power Distance Index

your turn!

MIND THE GAP

Power Distance Gap
Two ways you can shrink the gap?

_____

_____

5

RECOGNIZING GAPS TOOL

Tool in Brief
- **Physical Gaps** physical avoidance behavior can suggest a gap
- **Verbal Gaps** mitigated or indirect speech may express power distance
- **Behavioral Gaps** many times actions speak louder than words – watch for gaps between what someone says and what they do

TOOL IN PRACTICE

Use the tool to recognize signals of power distance. When you notice one use the discussion starters to help shrink the gap.

Physical Gaps
- Physical distance, turned toward an "exit"
- Avoiding eye contact, looking at ceiling
- Closed body language (arms crossed)
- Distracted, seems lost in thought
- Holding back or agitated body language

Behavioral Gaps
- Promising one thing, doing another
- No follow through or follow up
- Passive aggressive actions
- Being "too busy" or procrastinating
- "Changing mind" about importance of issue

Verbal Gaps... the most recognizable signals of power distance
- Watch for mitigated speech like **hints** ("I wonder if..."); **preference** ("perhaps we should..."); **question** ("do you think ___ would work?"); or **team suggestion** ("why don't we try ___?")
- Look for attempts to "sugarcoat" or downplay bad news
- Being overly polite or deferential
- Quickly deferring, backing down when rejected by someone in power

Discussion Starters... Once you notice a gap, try this to close it
"You seem uncomfortable. It's OK – I really want to know what you think."
"I'm not 100% sure what I think about this myself. Tell me what you really think."
"OK, that's what I do when I'm not sure if I should say something. What's up?"
"I need your help. Can you be honest and tell me exactly what you think about this?"
"I may be completely off base here... Can you tell me what you really think?"

ORGANIZATIONAL CITIZENSHIP

Organizational Citizenship
The tiny hinge that swings the big door on performance

Happy Employees = Happy Customers = Better Business?
WRONG: Satisfaction is a mediator

> *your turn!*
>
> **Can you name two Organizational Citizenship Behaviors?**
>
> _____
>
> _____

Organizational Citizenship Behavior (OCB) Predicts Performance

 **67%**

Organizational citizenship behaviors versus all other factors
Source: Cornell Hospitality Journal, 2010

What Predicts OCB? Approachable Supervisors.

 **88%**

Approachability predicts suggestions more than all other factors
Source: Journal of Management Development, 2005

THE CONNECTION MODEL

The Approachable Leadership® Connection Model

Be Open
right space

Understand
right feeling

Support
right action

Approachable Leadership Defined...

Connecting with another by being *welcoming*, and *seeking to understand* and (if possible) meet their *needs* and *desires*.

APPROACHABLE LEADERSHIP DEFINED

your turn!

What four "magic" words make you more approachable?

_____

_____

_____   _____

Great leaders create a space where you can bring your best to work each day.

Like a ring, leaders can be too loose or too tight. The best ones are there when you need them, gone when you don't.

KEY TAKEAWAYS: OPENNESS | RIGHT SPACE

Key Takeaways

- **Balance competence with warmth** – neither extreme is good
- **Unapproachable behavior has ripples** – impacts all future interactions
- **Unapproachable behavior often means:**
    - You'll always be "out of the loop"
    - People will avoid telling you things that are important (Power Distance, Air Florida)
    - Your team will feel unappreciated, disengaged, looking for the exit (unproductive, turnover)
- **Overly nice behavior often means:**
    - Your team won't trust you, feels fake or inauthentic
    - People feel like they aren't important or needed
    - People don't think you care (or understand) the business – low competence
- **"Just Right" behavior blends competence and warmth:**
    - Usually quicker and more efficient
    - Employee feels appreciated, needed, and understood
    - Employee more likely to approach in the future, give their best when they return, pitch in to help others

Openness Behaviors to Experiment with:

- Rearrange your office or work area.
- Check your body language (arms crossed often?)
- How fast do you walk?
- What's your typical resting facial expression?
- Work on your "first impression" – smile with your eyes
- Say "Hello, Please & Thank you."
- Notice and compliment organizational citizenship
- Look for signs of power distance (physical, verbal, behavioral)

COMMITMENT EXERCISE: PART 1
OPENNESS | RIGHT SPACE

Take a few minutes to complete the following. Discuss with your partner and then you will have a chance to share with the rest of the group.

Two openness behaviors I want to focus on

_____

_____

An obstacle that could get in my way

_____

_____

My plan to overcome that obstacle

_____

_____

The best research on habit formation finds that simply having a goal often fails. Instead, planning to overcome obstacles that might prevent you from reaching your goal dramatically increases the chance you'll follow through.

THE APPROACHABILITY WINDOW

your turn!

Two Approachability Strengths

_____

_____

Two Approachability Opportunities

_____

_____

Two "Blind" Spots (Strength and Opportunity)

_____

_____

APPROACHABILITY WINDOW

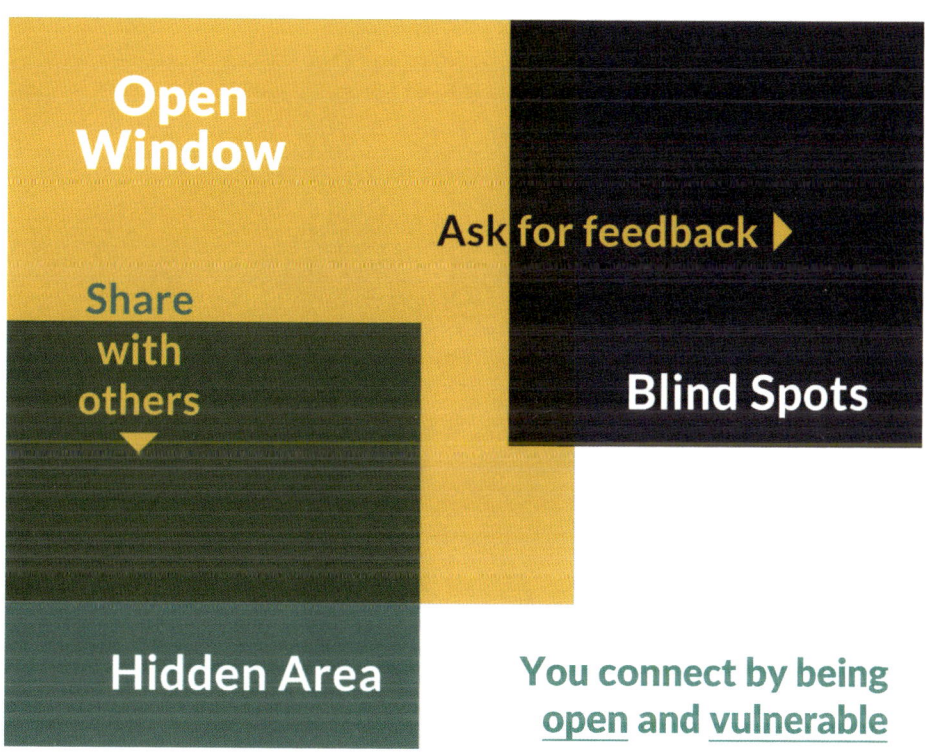

You connect by being *open* and *vulnerable*

Asking permission to give feedback
"Can I share something with you?"
"Can I tell you something I've noticed?"
"Can I check something out with you?"

How to Give Feedback
Permission + Hero Assumption
Observation + Impact
Full Stop + Discuss
Action + Follow Up

How to ask for feedback
"What can I do better?"
"Do I do anything that concerns you?"
"What advice would you give me?"

EMPATHY AND LISTENING

Stop. Listen. Confirm.
Only then collaborate to solve (sometimes)

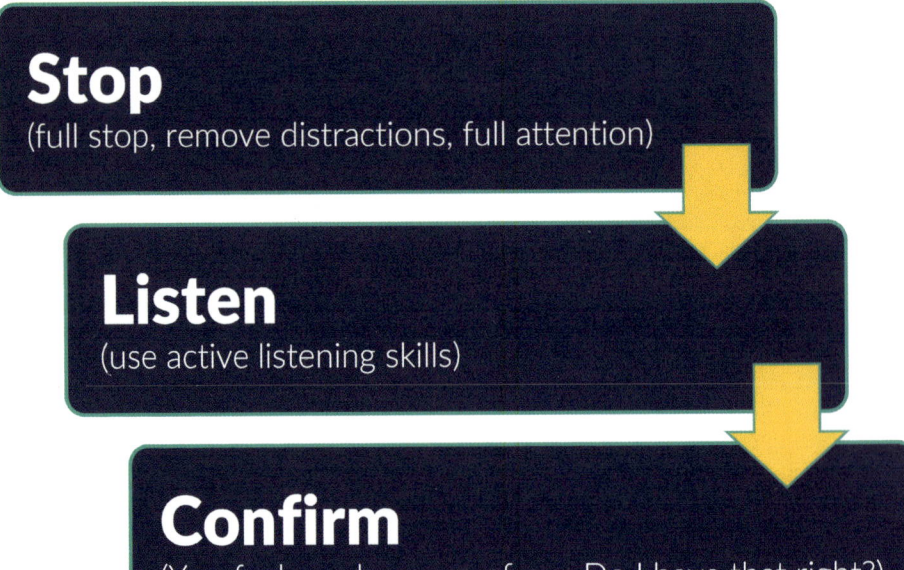

🚫 Don't use these! 🚫
Problem-focused questions

1. What's wrong?
2. Why do you have this problem?
3. Whose fault is it?
4. How long has this been going on?
5. What is this costing you?
6. Why haven't you overcome this problem?

Use These Instead!
Solution-focused questions

1. What result do we really want?
2. When can we start?
3. What do we need to get started?
4. What resources are available?
5. Who can help?
6. What can we begin doing now to get what we want?

ACTIVE LISTENING TOOL

Identify opportunities to improve your active listening skills. Use these *active listening phrases*:

Can you tell me more?
What does that look like?
I thought I heard you say... right?
You seem [emotion] about this...
What I hear you saying is...
Have you considered...
When you talk about this I noticed [behavior]...
You've obviously put a lot of effort into this...
Let me make sure I understand you....
Please tell me more about that...
That sounds like a great story, tell me more...
Is there anything else?

Pay Attention
(eye contact, not thinking about your response)

Show the speaker you are listening
(nonverbal, encourage, build, clarify, validate)

Provide feedback
(restate, reflect, summarize)

Don't judge
(encourage, validate)

Respond appropriately
(restate, validate, reflect)

Active Listening:
Pay Attention
Listening Behavior
Feedback
No Judgment
Respond

KEY TAKEAWAYS: UNDERSTANDING | RIGHT FEELING

Key Takeaways

- **Approachability Window**
    - You grow a relationship slowly – "offer and acceptance"
    - Ask for feedback about "blind spots"
    - Ask permission to offer feedback – always assume positive intent (the "Hero" assumption)
    - Remember how you felt giving and receiving the "yellow" card feedback – that's leadership
- **Stop-Listen-Confirm + Solution**
    - Focus on understanding <u>first</u>, then the solution
    - "Nobody cares how much you know until they know how much you care"
    - Be able to answer the "Confirm" statement (You feel [emotion] because of [situation]. Do I have that right?)
    - Don't ask problem-focused questions – ask solution-focused questions instead
- **Use Active Listening skills**
    - Listen with your whole body, not just your ears
    - Ask them to explain and clarify
    - Use open-ended questions
    - "Is there anything else?"

Understanding Behaviors to Experiment with:

- Pick an active listening behavior to practice
- Disclose something about yourself to another – wait for them to "accept" before offering more
- Try the "blue card/yellow card" exercise
- Practice using the "Confirm" statement
- Pick your favorite "solution-focused" question – ask it
- Ask for feedback from your direct reports
- Ask for feedback from your peers

COMMITMENT EXERCISE: PART 2
UNDERSTANDING | RIGHT FEELING

Take a few minutes to complete the following. Discuss with your partner and then you will have a chance to share with the rest of the group.

Two understanding behaviors I want to focus on

_____

_____

An obstacle that could get in my way

_____

_____

My plan to overcome that obstacle

_____

_____

The best research on habit formation finds that simply having a goal often fails. Instead, planning to overcome obstacles that might prevent you from reaching your goal dramatically increases the chance you'll follow through.

FOLLOW UP AND FOLLOW THROUGH

your turn!

What's your simple follow up tool or rule?

Your tool? _____

Your rule? _____

These are the 6 Key Areas for Follow Up and Follow Through.

How to Use Your Approachable Leadership Action + Leadership Journal

Use your *Action + Leadership Journal* each day to:

1. Be reminded about one key approachable leader behavior;
2. Express gratitude for three things in your life; and
3. Support your team by building effective follow-up and follow-through habits.

Tips on using your *Action + Leadership Journal*

Start Where You Are: This *Action + Leadership Journal* is designed to cover one month. If you like using the *Journal* you can order one that covers an entire quarter by calling 800-888-9115. You can then start over when a new quarter begins.

2 Pages Per Work Day: Each workday is covered by two pages. The *left-hand* page is where you review your approachable behavior for the week and journal about your three gratitudes. The *right-hand* page is your Action List (up to 10 actions per day) plus a notes area. Fill out a page for each day - carry over any open to-do items to the next day.

Markings: Your to-do list contains one box labelled "MIT" – this is your most important task. Commit to finish this task first and do your best not to carry it over. Here are a few other markings you can use (but see *Make it Your Own* below):

▨	Completed task	→	Moved/Didn't Complete
		←	Scheduled/Delegated (who?)
▧	In progress task	!	Important

Notes: The rest of the page is for notes. This is based on the "Cornell" note-taking method. Write your notes in the larger box and use the margin to summarize key points (date, time, attendees, key points or actions, etc.)

Make it Your Own: <u>There is no one way to do this</u>. Feel free to adjust anything to make it your own. Let us know any improvements you make!

And most important... Stay Approachable!

Week 1

FOCUS: Do You Have What You Need? | The Resource Question

> **Focus area** for this week. Work on building this one approachability behavior.

Gratitude	Really grateful for [...] the lake. Great to [...]
Gratitude	[...] a lot [...] healthy.
Gratitude	Great conversation with Tom yesterday about the issues on Line 12. He said he really appreciated the work I am doing on communicating better. Felt great.

> **Journal** briefly about three things you are thankful for in your life. This habit increases happiness, improves focus, builds empathy.

- Pre-shift 10/8/16
- Press
- Safety class
- Bins

- Pre-shift meeting 10/08/16
- All present
- Press down about 2 hours last night – need to work through breaks to make up lost production
- Safety class wasn't well attended, makeup class scheduled for next week. Told team they needed to be there
- Asked for feedback on the new placement of the materials bins – most everyone felt the new placement is a big improvement.
- Maintenance still feels like the bins are in the way of the controls area if they have to make adjustments.

> This is the **notes area**. This is where you will put detailed notes of any meetings or calls.

> **Summary area**. Put key details for each notes section here for quick reference. Summarizing will also help with your recall.

MIT	Talk to Frank about...
	Follow up with Tom on Line 12 issue
→	Ask Susan about bin placement - too close to controls?
	Talk to team about staggering breaks today
	Ask John Q2 (What would make work better?)
	Follow up with IT on John's computer reset time

Date goes here → 10 / 8 / 2016

Your **MIT (Most Important Task)** for the day. Commit to getting this done before you leave... try to avoid carrying it over.

Your other **tasks** for the day go here. You support others by being consistent at follow up and follow through. If you miss something carry it over to the next day.

NOTE: If a task is due in a future month, next year, or someday, log it in the back of your journal. Each month check these lists for tasks to add.

This is the **notes area**. This is where you will put detailed notes of any meetings or calls.

- Talked to John about Q2
- Problem with computer on his machine keeps re-setting at 2PM each day - wanted to know if that could be changed to a different time
- Told him I'd follow up with IT on whether that is something they can change

- Talk with John Q2

Summary area. Put key details for each notes section here for quick reference. Summarizing will also help with your recall.

KEY TAKEAWAYS
SUPPORT | RIGHT ACTION

Follow-Up Rules to Experiment with:
- Clean up your workspace each day before you leave.
- List your top three to-do items for next day before you leave.
- Empty your in-boxes (physical and virtual) each day and add follow-up items to your to-do list.
- Limit your in-boxes (one physical and one virtual in-box).
- Don't turn on your computer or tablet until you have taken a walk through the work area.
- Only check email at certain times each day.
- Arrive 30 minutes before your team to prepare for day.
- Make follow-up an agenda item for all meetings.
- Follow through on one to-do item before you wake up your computer each time you sit at your desk.
- Add follow-up to your morning or evening routine.

Supportive Environment Tools to Experiment with:
- Use an obvious, physical in-box where people know they can put items they want you to see.
- Use an "Always Around" in-box where you can capture follow-up items (a notebook, notecards, or a phone app are the most common).
- Use a "dictation" app so to-do items can be captured by voice (Siri® can add items to your reminders list or a document by just speaking them into your phone).
- Consider using a "location-aware" to-do app, that can remind you to take an action when you are in a certain location (like picking up a form when you are at the corporate office).
- Use a whiteboard to put your key to-do items, follow-up items, or issue-tracking system.
- Share an Excel® spreadsheet with your team so they can see progress on open items and when items close.

COMMITMENT EXERCISE: PART 3
SUPPORT | RIGHT ACTION

Two support behaviors I want to focus on

_____

_____

An obstacle that could get in my way

_____

_____

My plan to overcome that obstacle

_____

_____

The best research on habit formation finds that simply having a goal often fails. Instead, planning to overcome obstacles that might prevent you from reaching your goal dramatically increases the chance you'll follow through.

THE THREE QUESTIONS OF APPROACHABLE LEADERS

Three questions (and three assumptions) to begin your journey

THE THREE QUESTIONS OF APPROACHABLE LEADERS

Nobody thinks they are the villain of their story
The Hero Assumption
Pygmalion Effect

My job is to reduce frustration
The PITA Principle
The "F-Word" of Leadership

We all want to make progress
The Progress Principle

COMMITMENT EXERCISE

Step 1: My Co-Mentor: _____

    Phone and Email: _____

Step 2: Fill out your takeaway, impact, obstacle and plan in your *Action + Leadership Journal*:

- ☐ Review the actions you listed on your Openness (p. 11), Understanding (p. 17) and Support Commitments (p. 23). Pick your **top takeaway** from the Workshop, then list a positive impact you'll enjoy if you adopt it. Name a potential obstacle to adopting it. What's your plan to overcome that obstacle? Share with your Co-Mentor.
- ☐ Add a task to *your Action + Leadership Journal* to follow up with your Co-Mentor one week from today.

Step 3: Practice and use your Journal: Do the following each week:

- ☐ Fill out your *Action + Leadership Journal* each workday (follow the instructions on pages 19-21). Consider making a 15-minute calendar appointment to fill out your journal.
- ☐ Add a task to act on your **one takeaway** once per week.
- ☐ Add a task to act on any other commitments made for your "focus relationships" once per week.
- ☐ Add a task to check in with your Co-Mentor once each week.
- ☐ If any of these discussions generates an action item, add that as a task in your *Action + Leadership Journal*.
- ☐ Commit to following up on any action items by the end of the week.
- ☐ On the last day of each week write a quick note in the notes section in your *Action + Leadership Journal*. Answer:
    - ☐ How did you do on your commitments this week?
    - ☐ Did you learn anything? Is there anything you'd do different?

COMMITMENT EXERCISE

Take a few minutes to complete the following. Discuss with your Co-Mentor and then you will have a chance to share with the rest of the group.

My two "focus relationships" for the next 30 days

_____

_____

My <u>number one</u> takeaway from the *Workshop*

_____

What positive impact will this have on my leadership?

_____

_____

An obstacle that could get in my way

_____

My plan to overcome that obstacle

_____

The best research on habit formation finds that simply having a goal often fails. Instead, planning to overcome obstacles that might prevent you from reaching your goal dramatically increases the chance you'll follow through.

FOCUS: Capture | Capture should be easy, convenient, and always available.

Week 1

Gratitude

Gratitude

Gratitude

MIT	

Week 1

FOCUS: Capture | Capture should be easy, convenient, and always available.

Gratitude

Gratitude

Gratitude

MIT	

Week 1

FOCUS: Capture | Capture should be easy, convenient, and always available.

Gratitude

Gratitude

Gratitude

MIT

Week 1
FOCUS: Capture | Capture should be easy, convenient, and always available.

Gratitude

Gratitude

Gratitude

/ /

MIT	

Week 1
FOCUS: Capture | Capture should be easy, convenient, and always available.

Gratitude

Gratitude

Gratitude

MIT	

FOCUS: Organize | Identify what requires action or follow up.

Gratitude

Gratitude

Gratitude

/ /

MIT	

FOCUS: Organize | Identify what requires action or follow up.

Week 2

Gratitude

Gratitude

Gratitude

MIT	

Week 2

FOCUS: Organize | Identify what requires action or follow up.

Gratitude

Gratitude

Gratitude

MIT	

FOCUS: Organize | Identify what requires action or follow up.

Week 2

Gratitude

Gratitude

Gratitude

| MIT |

FOCUS: Organize | Identify what requires action or follow up.

Gratitude

Gratitude

Gratitude

/ /

MIT	

FOCUS: Prioritize | Important items get priority. Focus on your MIT.

Gratitude

Gratitude

Gratitude

MIT	

FOCUS: Prioritize | Important items get priority. Focus on your MIT.

Week 3

Gratitude

Gratitude

Gratitude

/   /

MIT	

FOCUS: Prioritize | Important items get priority. Focus on your MIT.

Week 3

Gratitude

Gratitude

Gratitude

MIT	

FOCUS: Prioritize | Important items get priority. Focus on your MIT.

Week 3

Gratitude

Gratitude

Gratitude

/ /

MIT

FOCUS: Prioritize | Important items get priority. Focus on your MIT.

Week 3

Gratitude

Gratitude

Gratitude

/ /

MIT

FOCUS: Execution | Limit distraction. Build momentum. Act. Start.

Week 4

Gratitude

Gratitude

Gratitude

/ /

MIT

FOCUS: Execution | Limit distraction. Build momentum. Act. Start.

Week 4

Gratitude

Gratitude

Gratitude

MIT

FOCUS: Execution | Limit distraction. Build momentum. Act. Start.

Week 4

Gratitude

Gratitude

Gratitude

MIT

FOCUS: Execution | Limit distraction. Build momentum. Act. Start.

Week 4

Gratitude

Gratitude

Gratitude

MIT

FOCUS: Execution | Limit distraction. Build momentum. Act. Start.

Week 4

Gratitude

Gratitude

Gratitude

MIT

13 KEY FOCUS AREAS
FOCUS ON 1 PER WEEK

This *Action + Leadership Journal* is designed to cover one month. If you like the *Journal* you can order one that covers an entire quarter by calling 800-888-9115.

Do You Have What You Need?	The resource question – assume people do their best with the resources they have.
What Would Make Work Better?	My job is to reduce friction – what can I do to reduce PITA factors.
Where Are You Going?	People want to make progress at work and in their lives.
The "Hero" Assumption	Nobody thinks they are the villain of their story; Remember the Pygmalion effect.
Power Distance	Look for gaps - "shrink the gap" with those in a lower power position – make them comfortable.
PITA Principle	Your job is to reduce friction for your team. Look for everyday frustrations you can fix.
Progress Principle	People want to make progress. What are you doing to help develop your team?
Approachability Window	We grow relationships by sharing vulnerably and seeking feedback.
Stop, Listen, Confirm+Collaborate (Understanding)	Empathize, Listen Actively: "You feel ___ because of ___, do I have that right?" – Only then use solution-focused questions.
Curb Appeal (Openness)	Make yourself and your space inviting and welcoming to others.
Follow Up Rules and Tools (Support)	You're holding one in your hand – recommit to using your tools and rules.
Organizational Citizenship Behavior	People go above and beyond for leaders and teammates they appreciate.
Reflection	Where are you going? How have you progressed in your leadership?

The Approachable Leadership® Connection Model

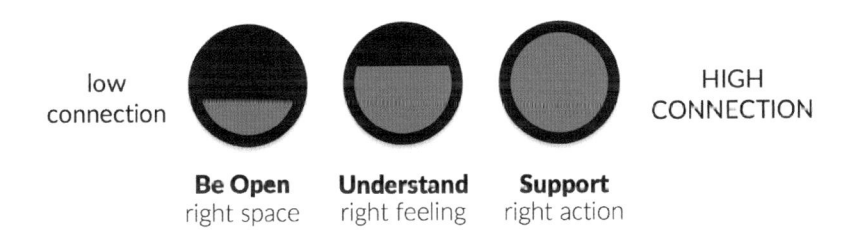

low connection — **Be Open** right space — **Understand** right feeling — **Support** right action — HIGH CONNECTION

The Connection Model describes how leaders can use approachable behavior to build connection with coworkers. Here's how we define Approachable Leadership:

Approachable leaders connect with others by being *Open, Understanding, and Supportive.* These behaviors form the three pillars of Approachable Leadership.

Each of these behaviors is expressed through habits you can learn and practice every day. Approachable Leaders show:
- *Openness* by being available, welcoming, and inviting—creating and maintaining "Right Space."
- *Understanding* through warmth, active listening, and empathy—exhibiting "Right Feeling."
- *Support* by being receptive to others, then following up and following through—performing "Right Action."

See page 27 of The Approachability Playbook

About Approachable Leadership

At *Approachable Leadership* our mission is to help you tackle 3 major challenges facing most businesses today:
- The *Cooperation Gap* (**3/4** of all change projects fail, and **53%** of those projects destroy value);
- the *Enthusiasm Gap* (**71%** of employees are disengaged, costing companies **$550 billion**); and
- the *Talent Gap* (**20%** of workers will voluntarily quit this year, costing businesses **$11 billion**).

These issues are stumbling blocks to success. Many companies mistakenly attack these challenges with a "whack-a-mole" approach that drains resources and energy.

How does Approachability address these challenges?
- Approachable leaders see **88% more "above and beyond" behavior** from their teams.
- Employees with Approachable leaders are **89% more likely to be engaged**.
- Turnover intention **decreases by 71%**.

To learn more about Approachable Leadership and becoming a more approachable leader visit: http://ApproachableLeadership.com or call us at 800-888-9115

Made in the USA
Columbia, SC
21 March 2018